25730   Jnf Biog

jB SIT
Viola, Herman J.
Sitting Bull / text by
Herman J. Viola ;
illustrations by Charles
Shaw.

PO Box 20
202 Main Street
Lakeview, Iowa 51450

To the Reader . . .

The **Raintree/Rivilo American Indian Stories** series
features the lives of American Indian men and women
important in the history of their tribes. Our purpose is to
provide young readers with accurate accounts of the lives of
these individuals. The stories are written by scholars, including
American Indians.

Indians are as much a part of American life today as they
were one hundred years ago. Even in times past, Indians were
not all the same. Not all of them lived in tepees or wore feather
warbonnets. They were not all warriors. Some did fight against
the white man, but many befriended him.

Whether patriot or politician, athlete or artist, Arapaho or
Zuni, the story of each person in this series deserves to be told.
Whether the individuals gained distinction on the battlefield or
the playing field, in the courtroom or the classroom, they have
enriched the heritage and history of all Americans. It is hoped
that those who read their stories will realize that many different
peoples, regardless of culture or color, have played a part in
shaping the United States, in making America the great country
that it is today.

Herman J. Viola
General Editor
Author of *Exploring the West*
and other volumes on the West
and American Indians

GENERAL EDITOR
Herman J. Viola
Author of *Exploring the West* and other volumes on the West
and American Indians

MANAGING EDITOR
Robert M. Kvasnicka
Coeditor of *The Commissioners of Indian Affairs, 1824–1977*
Coeditor of *Indian-White Relations: A Persistent Paradox*

MANUSCRIPT EDITOR
Barbara J. Behm

DESIGNER
Kathleen A. Hartnett

PRODUCTION
Andrew Rupniewski
Eileen Rickey

First Steck-Vaughn Edition 1992

Copyright © 1990 Pinnacle Press, Inc. doing business as Rivilo
Books

Library of Congress Number: 89-10372

3 4 5 6 7 8 9   97 96 95 94 93 92

Library of Congress Cataloging-in-Publication Data

Viola, Herman J.
  Sitting Bull.
  (Raintree American Indian stories)
  Summary: A biography of the American Indian who engineered
the defeat of Custer and his troops at Little Big Horn and toured
with Buffalo Bill's Wild West Show.
  1. Sitting Bull, 1831-1890—Juvenile literature.   2. Dakota
Indians—Biography—Juvenile literature.   3. Indians of North
America—Great Plains—Biography—Juvenile literature.   [1. Sitting
Bull, 1831-1890.   2. Dakota Indians—Biography.   3. Indians of
North America—Great Plains—Biography.]   I. Title.   II. Series.
E99.D1S6272   1989   978'.00497502   [B]   [92]   89-10372
ISBN 0-8172-3401-2 (lib. bdg.)

AMERICAN INDIAN STORIES

SITTING BULL

Text by Herman J. Viola
Illustrations by Charles Shaw

RAINTREE
STECK-VAUGHN
L I B R A R Y
Austin, Texas

Sitting Bull is one of the most famous Indians in American history. The reasons for this are many. He was a warrior, a statesman, a showman, and a holy man, but above all, he was a fighter. As a young man, Sitting Bull fought to protect his family and his Sioux people from their enemies. As an old man, he fought to protect their way of life from change.

The Sioux Indians, or Lakota, were once one of the most powerful tribes of North America. They were so large that the tribe had many bands. The band to which Sitting Bull belonged was the Hunkpapa.

The Sioux were fearless hunters who roamed over much of the Great Plains in search of the bison, or buffalo, which was their primary source of food. They usually hunted the buffalo from horseback using spears and bows and arrows. The meat of these mighty creatures provided the Sioux with much of their food. The hides were made into tepee covers and blankets. The bones and horns became tools, cups, and rattles. The Sioux used every part of the buffalo, wasting nothing. Even the manure, called chips, was used instead of wood to make camp fires.

The buffalo gave the Sioux their strength and livelihood, but it was the horse that gave them their freedom and spirit. How the Sioux loved their horses! Each family owned many of them. The Sioux needed many horses to carry all their belongings when they followed the buffalo. Since a good horse was a warrior's most prized possession, he would keep it next to his tepee at night so that enemy Indians, like the Assiniboin, the Blackfeet, and the Crow, could not steal it.

Sitting Bull was born in March 1831 at a place called Many-Caches, which is in present-day South Dakota. His father was a brave warrior named *Jumping Bull.* Jumping Bull was very proud of his newborn son, whom he first named *Slow. Slow* seemed a good name for the baby because he seemed to think very carefully before doing anything, even when eating and walking.

Until the age of ten, Slow enjoyed the life of a typical Sioux boy. Parents seldom punished or scolded their children, who were always surrounded by uncles, aunts, and grandparents. The relatives not only loved, teased, and spoiled the children, but they also taught them important lessons.

Sioux children learned tribal stories from their families. They learned how to behave properly. They learned to accept hardships without complaining, to be generous to one another, and to understand that the Great Spirit had placed the plants and animals on the earth for everyone to share and use. Girls learned how to find the tastiest berries and roots and how to skin animals and prepare fine leather clothes. Boys learned to shoot a bow and arrow from horseback, to ride the most spirited horses, and to slay the fearsome buffalo.

In Sioux society, being a famous warrior was like being a star athlete on a football or basketball team today. Warriors earned honors and special praise for brave deeds such as touching an enemy in battle or sneaking into an enemy village at night to capture one of their prize horses that was tied to a tepee. These brave deeds were called *coups,* which is a French word meaning "triumph." Sometimes a warrior would receive an eagle feather from his relatives for a successful coup. Important warriors like Sitting Bull often got so many eagle feathers that they would make warbonnets to wear in battle. These warbonnets of eagle feathers identified them as great fighters, and their enemies would try even harder to catch them.

Sitting Bull was only ten years old when he counted his first coup. This was young, even for a Sioux boy, but Sitting Bull was no ordinary boy. When he saw his father preparing his equipment to join a war party against their Crow enemies, Slow decided to go along even though he did not have permission. Many of the men were annoyed at his boldness, but they let him tag along. His father, however, was very proud of him and gave him a special wand to carry called a coup stick. Slow was to touch an enemy with it, if he got close enough.

Instead of being a hero, Slow almost caused a disaster. After traveling many days, the Sioux warriors came across a Crow war party riding toward them. The Sioux planned an ambush by hiding in some bushes and attacking when the Crow warriors came alongside. Slow, however, was too excited to wait. As soon as he saw the Crow, he charged. The rest of the Sioux war party had no choice but to follow him. The Crow warriors immediately turned their horses and tried to gallop away, but Slow was right behind the slowest rider. The Crow warrior tried to surprise Slow by stopping his horse, dismounting, and shooting an arrow at him. But the plan did not work. Slow whipped the warrior with the coup stick as he galloped past and knocked him down. Before the startled warrior could get up, the rest of the Sioux war party rode up and killed him.

When the Sioux warriors got back to their village, Jumping Bull gave his son a fine bay-colored horse and a new name. "My son has struck the enemy!" the proud father shouted to the excited villagers. "He is brave! I now change his name to *Ta-tan'-ka I-yo-ta'-ke,* Sitting Bull!"

As Sitting Bull grew older, his world began to change. New people were coming into Sioux country. These people had white skin and strange ways. Sitting Bull marveled at their large wagons pulled by lumbering creatures called oxen, but he did not like the strangers. They built houses, cut up the earth for gardens, and scared the buffalo away. Sitting Bull at first tried to avoid the white people. Later, he tried to frighten them away, but they would not leave. Instead, the settlers and soldiers continued to arrive in increasing numbers.

The 1860s were troubled times for all the Sioux bands. After the Civil War, thousands of white people moved onto the Sioux homelands. Many of these settlers were immigrants from foreign countries who wanted to start a new life in America. They hoped to live in peace with the Indians, but misunderstandings led to warfare. Soon there was fighting over much of the Great Plains. The Sioux, as well as the Cheyenne, Arapaho, Comanche, Kiowa, and other tribes were at war with the white people.

Sitting Bull was, at that time, in his thirties and an important tribal leader with many wives and children. He tried to avoid the fighting by keeping his village far away from railroads and towns. He also refused to sign any treaties with the United States government or to talk to any government officials because he knew they wanted to put him and his people on a reservation. A reservation is a tract of land set aside as a safe place for Indians to live. But Indians thought of the reservations as prisons because they had to abandon all of their customs and they were confined to a single area. The Indians who lived there were expected to learn white ways and to stop hunting and roaming the plains. They were to become farmers, wear clothes like the white people, speak English, and practice the religion of white people.

Sitting Bull did not want to learn white ways. "I am a red man," he said. "If the Great Spirit had desired me to be a white man, he would have made me so in the first place. It is not necessary for eagles to be crows. Now we are poor but we are free."

Sitting Bull's feelings toward reservations were equally strong. "I do not wish to be shut up in a corral. It is bad for young men to be fed by an Indian agent," he said. "All agency Indians I have seen were worthless. They are neither red warriors nor white farmers. They are neither wolf nor dog."

Sitting Bull avoided serious trouble until 1874. That year, however, a government expedition went exploring in the Black Hills, which are sacred to the Sioux people even today. The man who led the expedition was Lieutenant Colonel George Armstrong Custer of the United States Cavalry. Custer was a hero of the Civil War and a famous Indian fighter. Unfortunately for the Sioux, Custer found gold in the Black Hills. When the news became public, hundreds of gold miners rushed onto the sacred hunting grounds of the Sioux. Sitting Bull knew the time to fight had come.

Although many Sioux bands were at this time on reservations, their young men were still anxious to earn honors in battle. When they learned that Sitting Bull wanted to drive the white people from the Black Hills, hundreds of warriors went to his village on the Little Big Horn River in what is today southeastern Montana. By June 1876, Sitting Bull's village was one of the largest ever seen on the Northern Plains. No one knows the exact numbers, but there may have been as many as 5,000 warriors and 25,000 horses in the encampment.

Sitting Bull had many warriors, but still he was worried. Could he really hope to defeat the white man's army? To find out, he underwent the Sun Dance. This was the most important religious ceremony of the Sioux people. Only the bravest and strongest men could endure it because the dancers had to go without food and water for three days. During this time, the men were attached to a tall post by long leather strings tied to the skin on their chests or backs. As they danced, they had to pull the strings through their skin. Although it was very painful, the dancers could not cry or act like it hurt.

During the ceremony, Sitting Bull lost consciousness and had a vision in which he saw a large army attacking his village. The soldiers were not normal, however. They were all upside down. When Sitting Bull awoke, he knew what the vision meant. The soldiers were all dead, and the Sioux were going to win a great victory.

Sitting Bull's prediction came true on June 25, 1876. On that day, the Seventh Cavalry, led by Custer himself, attacked Sitting Bull's huge village on the Little Big Horn River. Although the Sioux were surprised, they remembered Sitting Bull's prediction and quickly overcame Custer and his soldiers. By the end of the day, Custer and more than two hundred of his soldiers were dead. The Sioux, with their Cheyenne and Arapaho allies, had won a great victory. It was so one-sided that only a dozen or so Indians had been killed.

After this victory, Sitting Bull thought that the United States government would leave him alone. Instead, the victory only made things worse. The army wanted revenge, and it attacked all Indians not yet on reservations. As the months passed, many of Sitting Bull's followers surrendered. Winter was especially hard on the Sioux. They were cold and did not have an abundance of food to eat. Their horses were also undernourished and weak. The army attacked the Indians mainly in winter because the soldiers knew that these harsh conditions made the Indians more willing to surrender. At least on reservations, the Sioux could stay warm, have food to eat, and be safe from attack.

No matter how difficult things became, however, Sitting Bull refused to surrender. Once, when soldiers got too close to his village, he sent them this message: "You scare all the buffalo away. I want to hunt in this place. I want you to turn back from here. If you don't, I will fight you again."

Since the soldiers wanted Sitting Bull most of all, they kept chasing him. Finally, with no place left to hide, the stubborn leader made a difficult decision. Rather than surrender, he left the United States. Less than one year after defeating Custer, the Hunkpapa Sioux left the land of their ancestors and crossed the border into Canada.

23

In Canada, they were safe from the soldiers, but it was a hard life. The weather was very cold, and they had very little to eat because white hunters had killed all the buffalo. Sitting Bull's people were hungry and homesick. Many of them—even one of Sitting Bull's daughters—left his village and secretly joined friends and relatives on reservations in the United States. Finally, in July 1881, Sitting Bull himself made the decision to return. "I will fight no more," he said. "Now all my people want to return to their native land. They wish to see their brothers and their old home. Therefore, I bow my head and submit."

It made Sitting Bull very sad to accept the new way of life that he had fought so hard to avoid. He and his people were placed on the Standing Rock Reservation in Dakota Territory.

Because of the battle with Custer, Sitting Bull became a very famous person in the United States. So many people wanted to see him and get his autograph that the government allowed him to join Buffalo Bill's Wild West Show. Buffalo Bill, whose real name was William F. Cody, had been a pony express rider, army scout, and buffalo hunter. He realized that many Americans who lived in the cities wanted to see real cowboys and Indians, so he organized a circus that traveled around the United States.

Sitting Bull agreed to join so he could get more food and help for his people. He even wrote a letter to President Grover Cleveland, using the stationery from the Wild West Show, but he never got an answer.

Being with the Wild West Show made Sitting Bull very happy. He enjoyed the applause of the crowds and the money he received from his autographs. He also liked helping to put up the "big top," the large circus tent in which the show was held. But most of all he liked Annie Oakley, a girl who did trick shooting with a rifle. Sitting Bull named her "Little Sure Shot" and tried to adopt her. Even when grumpy, he would always smile at the dance she performed after her act.

Sitting Bull stayed with the circus one year. When he left, Buffalo Bill gave him a special present—a beautiful horse that could do tricks.

When Sitting Bull returned to the Standing Rock Reservation, he found that his people were still very unhappy. They did not like the reservation. They wanted to live as they had in the old days. That is why many of them joined a new Indian religion called the Ghost Dance. The believers were called Ghost Dancers because they wore white shirts made from flour sacks. The Ghost Dancers prayed to the Great Spirit to bring back the buffalo and send the white people away. This made the white people afraid because they thought the Ghost Dancers meant to kill them.

When Sitting Bull became a believer in the new religion, the government decided to arrest him. Early one morning as the old man lay asleep in his cabin with his wives and children, the

Indian police came for him. While trying to put him on the horse given to him by Buffalo Bill, the policemen made too much noise and awakened Sitting Bull's followers, who came running from their tepees. Soon the policemen were surrounded by angry Indians. "Let him go!" they yelled. Everyone was tense and nervous. Suddenly someone fired a gun, and a terrible battle took place. Within a few minutes, fourteen men were killed. One of them was Sitting Bull.

A strange thing happened during the gun battle. Sitting Bull's horse thought it was back in the Wild West Show and began doing tricks. When the Indians saw this, they stopped shooting because they thought Sitting Bull's spirit had gone into his horse.

Sitting Bull died on December 15, 1890. The Ghost Dance religion among the Sioux died two weeks later when many of Sitting Bull's followers and other Sioux believers were killed by the cavalry at a place called Wounded Knee. Although some tribes continued to practice the religion, no one really believed the old days would return.

Sitting Bull was a great leader. Although he has been dead for a century, his spirit can be seen in those American Indians today who are working hard to keep their language and culture alive. Sitting Bull is also a symbol to people everywhere who resist oppression and who fight for freedom. "No man controls our footsteps," he once declared. "If we must die, we die defending our rights."

HISTORY OF SITTING BULL

1831   Sitting Bull was born and was given the name *Slow*. Ex-President John Quincy Adams began serving the first of eight terms in the House of Representatives.

1841   Slow counted his first coup, and was renamed *Sitting Bull.*

1874   Lieutenant Colonel George Armstrong Custer led a government expedition exploring the Black Hills and discovered gold.

1876   The battle of the Little Bighorn took place. The United States celebrated its 100th birthday as a nation.

1877   Sitting Bull and his people moved to Canada rather than surrender to the government.

1881   Sitting Bull and his people returned from Canada and were placed on the Standing Rock Reservation in Dakota Territory.

1885   Sitting Bull toured with Buffalo Bill's Wild West Show. The Washington Monument in Washington, D.C., was dedicated.

1890   Sitting Bull was killed when Indian police attempted to arrest him because of his support of the Ghost Dance religion.